Birdhouse Plans

11 DIY Bird House Building Ideas You Can Build to Attract and Retain Birds Plus Tools, Placement and Maintenance Tips to Get You Started

By

Phil Yates

Copyright © 2021 – Phil Yates

All rights reserved

No part of this publication may be reproduced, distributed, or transmitted in any form or by any means, including photocopying, recording, or other electronic or mechanical methods, without the prior written permission of the publisher, except in the case of brief quotations embodied in reviews and certain other non-commercial uses permitted by copyright law.

Disclaimer

This publication is designed to provide competent and reliable information regarding the subject matter covered. However, the views expressed in this publication are those of the author alone, and should not be taken as expert instruction or professional advice. The reader is responsible for his or her own actions.

The author hereby disclaims any responsibility or liability whatsoever that is incurred from the use or application of the contents of this publication by the purchaser or reader. The purchaser or reader is hereby responsible for his or her own actions.

Table of Contents

Introduction 6

Chapter 1 10

Essentials of Birdhouse Building 10

    What Is a Birdhouse? 10

    History of The Birdhouse 14

    Importance of Building a Birdhouse 17

Chapter 2 26

Birdhouse Construction Basics 26

Chapter 3 38

Bird House Building Tips 38

Chapter 4 51

Getting Started with Birdhouse Buildings 51

    Tools and Supplies 51

        Wood 51
        Fasteners and Glue 55
        Handsaw 56
        Chisel 56

Hand-Powered Drill 57
Drill or Driver 57
Drill Bits 57
Jigsaw 58
Hole Saw Set 58
Hammer 58
Tape Measure 59
Clamps 59
T-Square 59
Screwdriver 59
Keeping Birdhouse Safe From Predators 60

Predator Guards and Its Importance 65

Placement of Birdhouse 67

Monitoring and Cleaning the Birdhouse 71

Chapter 5 74

Birdhouse Plans and Ideas 74

Simple Birdhouse 75

Fence Picket Birdhouse 81

Modern Birdhouse 84

Beginner Birdhouse 87

License Plates Birdhouse 90

Songbird Birdhouse 94

Sparrow Birdhouse Box 98

Peanut Butter Birdhouse 100

Gourd Birdhouse 103

Natural Log Birdhouse 107

Cardboard Birdhouse 110

Chapter 6 115

Common Problems With Building Birdhouses 115

Conclusion 128

Introduction

Have you heard what they say about loving nature? A wise man once said, "if you love nature, you will find beauty everywhere." Have you stood outside your house early in the morning and paid attention to the chirpings or sweet whistling of songbirds and watch how they light up the sky when they fly? If you have paid attention to nature, you would definitely have to appreciate the beauty that this set of creatures bring to the world. Steve Maraboli also made a memorable quote on nature, "plant seeds of happiness, hope, success, and love; it will all come back to you in abundance. This is the law of nature." Hence, if you are a lover of nature and its beauty, it would make sense to you the importance of building a birdhouse.

Birds are known to make their own dwelling place; this is one very interesting thing about them. They make their nest with twigs in very quiet places, on very tall heights. Although some cavity nesters lived inside broken tree trunks for several years, most species of birds created their own nests on rooftops, abandoned furniture, rusty shelves, or treetops. This nest usually houses them and their chicks during the nesting season.

However, it is destructible, fragile and prone to damage. Every time their nests get destroyed, they would have to relocate to a new location and rebuild. Most birds like to nest in dark cupboards or very cold and quiet corners. Birds don't like to stay in a hot or uncomfortable place; they place value on their comfort and safety. To birds, comfort is a quiet, cool, reserved corner. You can't see a bird nest in a busy or noisy place.

When you purchase a bird as a pet for yourself, you won't wait for the bird to build its own place when you can actually make for it somewhere comfier and more secured. Hence, you wouldn't have to bother about waste management, feeding convenience, and the security of the bird.

To make having a bird pet easier and possible, the birdhouse was invented. The birdhouse is made from wood, so it doesn't tamper with the bird's comfort. They could still nest inside the birdhouse, but it gives them more warmth and security.

However, there are different styles of birdhouses built for different types of birds. It is not uncommon to find one birdhouse that can house two or different species of birds, but it is more comfortable and safer when you use specific measurements and models to build for respective birds.

Talking about safety, just the way the eco system is created, birds are potential prey to many predators, the same way they happen to feed on insects. Hence, the security and comfort of the birdhouse must be prioritized above designs when building.

Building birdhouses can be quite exhilarating and stressful all the same; however, it makes like a great team project. You can make a simple birdhouse with the help of your kids, family and neighbors. Asides from making birdhouses or nest boxes as it is called to house your pet, you could also place it in your yard to house visiting birds. This way, you would be helping to make the environment a safer place for them, and in a way, it also adds a sort of glamour to your yard.

Scientists have it that over the last three decades or more, the population of birds is drastically reducing. It could be due to deforestation, modernization, disruptions, human carelessness, or activities, amongst other reasons.

Some species of birds have gotten totally extinct, according to history. However, the birdhouse can solve this problem in many ways. We will look at them in this coming chapter.

Even though you don't want to rear a bird, you could just build a habitat for it in your garden where it can live and tend its young. This little quota of yours can positively affect the eco system and help establish the existence of birds in the environment.

The birdhouse can be used to host an avian population of birds and help them have a stable reproductive site.

We would be looking at the different birdhouse plans for specific popular birds, that is majorly what this book is about, and we would be checking that out in the coming chapters.

Let's get started!

Chapter 1

Essentials of Birdhouse Building

What Is a Birdhouse?

The birdhouse is a small box or nest used to shelter birds. It is usually a large enclosure used to house birds. It can also be called a nestbox.

In some fashion, it is also a little house built for birds to live in. They sometimes look like real person's houses, except that they come in a very small size, fit for only a bird to live in.

The birdhouse is addressed as an aviary. In some places, the aviary is always well beautified and decorated to display birds in exhibition shows. In public festivals and ceremonies, these special boxes are termed exhibition boxes.

Whether for exhibition or not, the birdhouse is a shelter box or nest for housing birds. The nest box is a manmade enclosure; it has the exact shape of a box, except for its slanted top, which is made in the shape of a roof to look like a real house.

This birdhouse can be used to shelter different types of birds, including the mammalian species known as bats.

Asides from the exhibition, and the beautification reason I have mentioned already, people build nests for different reasons. Similarly, they keep all kinds of bird species for special reasons in reserve centers. The way it is operational in the zoo, people place nest boxes to help secure and preserve a particular species of bird. It is also used to help maintain a population range of a particular species for exhibition or nature's sake.

This house is usually made from wood for many reasons. Several years before modernization hit man and many things began to be reformed, birds used to live in nests made from twigs and little sticks fallen from trees. This nest, they also built on the tree.

So, if you would be replacing an assemble of twigs for a new shelter, it only makes sense that you build with their own material. The wood is very comfortable for them.

It is quite porous and allows for enough moisture and heat during weather changes. This is one thing other materials like plastic and metal cannot regulate. They can be affected adversely by heat, hence affecting the bird. The wood appears to be the safest material to use, and it is also more durable.

Asides from the material, there are several other things to consider when building a birdhouse. They will be discussed fully in the coming chapters. It actually costs almost nothing to build a birdhouse. It doesn't require so much finance and time investment. In an hour or less, your birdhouse is ready, depending on the model of birdhouse you are making. You don't have to be an expert; all you need is the right measure of knowledge, which will be unfolded in the subsequent pages of this book.

Research has it that many birds would choose to stay in an enclosed place, and it only makes sense to give them an alternative habitat as their natural habitat is being dominated by the day.

The birdhouse provides a valuable opportunity for birdwatchers to enjoy watching their birds; it allows for exhibition in popular places. Also, they provide standard homes for birds. It is just like the improvement from thatch house to wood. You can't compare the difference or the advantages it holds over the former option.

Also, the birdhouse happens to be a very more comfortable habitat because it shields the birds from harsh temperatures like sunlight and rain. Most birds like the Eastern bluebirds, chickadees, Barred owls, nuthatches, wrens, Screech owls and woodpeckers love to have roofs over their heads to help them regulate the harsh atmosphere or temperature from affecting the bird.

This way, the life span of the bird is more preserved and its habitat is made safer.

The birdhouse has to be modified to meet the bird's preference. Every type of bird will want to have a very comfortable space. Well, we do have a whole long list of different species. You have to understand the specification for the type of bird you want to attract to your yard.

Birdhouses commonly come in plain dull and natural colors; it makes the birds feel safer as bright colors scream predation.

Some conservationists usually position the nest box in strategic places where they can easily attract specific bird types. Hence, the design, positioning, and shape of the birdhouse must be considered in relation to the bird's preference if that is your goal or aim of making the birdhouse. Also to consider is the color of the birdhouse. I have mentioned that birds appreciate natural colors more; however, you also have to consider whether you are making an indoor or outdoor birdhouse. You have to choose a model or color that fits your outdoor or indoor background theme. You might also have to look out for a design that matches the design of your house.

History of The Birdhouse

The word birdhouse originated in 1865-70. It is an American word that was formed by adding BIRD to HOUSE.

Birdhouse is a part of western culture; they have been so for a very long time. Ever since the first man-made birdhouse was used in Turkey, it has transited from a simple domestic tool to a copula and highly reverenced cultural material. I bet you didn't know this. The birdhouse has been existing as a cultural tool.

Before this time, the dwelling place of birds was addressed as nests. Birds were said to build nests on tree branches, gutters, and porches, just anywhere that allowed them to have their cool and quiet moment.

Many birds still make their abode in these places today, but it has been established that that isn't safe for them.

While some birds build their nests themselves from scratch by gathering figs and twigs, some birds look out for holes in wood where they can build their nests. This category of birds are called cavity nesters. Unfortunately for them, there are hardly enough holes to go around, so they are rendered homeless or have to scout for a very long time in an uncomfortable habitat. This is what makes the birdhouse a very good option for bird's nesting.

The first man-made birdhouse was made and used in the 15th -16th century in Turkey. However, it wasn't long before that invention was forgotten.

The birdhouse was again brought to invention in the early 19th century by a British conservationist named Charles Waterton. He was inspired to invent the birdhouse to encourage birdlife and wildfowl in reserves like the natural reserve he was working with. This invention in no time became widely adopted by many reserve centers.

Before the invention, birds were kept in iron cages to keep them from escaping, but the birdhouse appeared to be a better and comfier alternative. Therefore, it wasn't difficult for many persons to accept it, judging from the fact that it appeared to be the best option. Although, some people try to argue if the birdhouse was a better shelter than the nests the animals built themselves. This argument didn't last a while before the debaters got to appreciate it themselves. Many years later, there were several modifications to the invention by different people who wanted to satisfy their adventurous spirit or just give expression to their own designs or concept life.

One of them was the traditional nest boxes that have been existing for many years through many civilizations. However, the modern nest boxes have fully overshadowed their existence today, except in native places like Columbia and Guinea. These modern nest boxes are becoming more popular because of the increase in industrialization, modern construction methods, and urban growth. In recent times, there has been a sharp decline in bird's natural habitats; a French conservationist observed this. He further mentioned that the decline is a result of deforestation, which renders most birds homeless.

Hence, the birdhouse is a very good way of preserving the birds from extinction. In others words, a birdhouse is a tool used to prevent bird extinction.

Importance of Building a Birdhouse

There are so many benefits of building a birdhouse, but they all fall in the category of reasons why you build a birdhouse.

- Some build birdhouses to attract birds to their house.
- Others build birdhouses to trap birds and train them as pets or to be sold.
- Birdhouses are also built as decorative boxes for bird exhibitions.

However, the importance and benefits of owning a birdhouse are listed below.

1. If you are a lover of birds and desire to have some of these beautiful creatures gracing your yard, then you should consider owning a birdhouse. It is an attractive force that encourages them to keep coming around or stay permanently. It is a perfect replacement for the local bird nests that these birds make themselves on trees, as it is comfier. It

attracts the birds and makes them keep visiting, as every bird will want to stay in a place that is well comfortable for them. This benefit is for only those that love the idea of hosting birds and still allowing them to roam freely.

If you are not a bird lover, these creatures' consistent visits and exits could piss you off. Remember, birds are joyful and happy creatures. They move with their ambience everywhere they go.

2. Also, birdhouses provide a safe habitat for birds to build their nests. A habitat is safe from harsh weather conditions, predators, and elements. Although birds love to have their freedom and move about in their own freewill, they still desire to have their own safety in harsh conditions. In very harsh weather conditions like winter, the birdhouse provides the birds a place to snuggle and be warm safe from the cold air. This way, you can add your own quarter to the eco system by sharing a little part of your habitat with birds. Trust nature to reward your kindness.

Before we look at the benefits of having a birdhouse, let's look at the benefit of having the birds around. It is not new that birds generally perform very dynamic roles in society and the eco system in particular. There are several functions that birds perform that keep the eco system running healthily. As insignificant as they might appear, without them, the structure of the animal system will be incomplete.

3. Birds are also known to help in controlling pests. They are classified as insectivores. Birds feed on pests and insects that could be harmful to your surroundings or crops. Having them in the garden or around the yard could eliminate these harmful pests that threaten to destroy your crops or tamper with your health. This is a healthier option than chemical pesticides, and you don't have to be afraid of the birds eating your crops. They don't eat crops. They help to control insect existence that could get out of hand if not controlled.

4. Also, birds assist in flower pollination. Birds are great pollination agents. They help in carrying nectar from one flower to another, thereby making pollination possible and effective. They make a good replacement for bees which happens to be one of the most effective pollination agents. Hence, they help to grow the economy of your garden. Building the birdhouse in the garden or around the house ensures that they are closer to you and able to help you pollinate.

5. Birds help in weed control. They love to eat weed seeds. Hence reducing the possibility of the weed germinating and spreading. This reduces the weeding job for the gardener, as the weeds are also reduced. In other words, I can choose to say that having birds around reduces your gardening chores.

6. As I have already mentioned, there is this ambiance that birds carry around. Having them around sparks up in the place in one kind of way. Whether they are pets or not, they help to keep the ambiance lively and tidy in a way. Just

imagine how our world would be without song birds. They give pleasure and calmness at the same time. Nothing can give you such a feeling. Just imagine that you awaken and there is no chirping bird or singing owl; life would look so weird. They complete the ecosystem and helps to maintain it also. Before music became very conventional, most persons were used to singing birds, especially those who live in tropical areas. They make us feel at peace with nature. Even while we live our busy lives, the sound of the song bird helps us feel calm and at peace not just with ourselves but with nature. Indeed, not all birds are songbirds, but all birds make sounds that we can easily identify and trace to them. They make sounds like chirping, chipping, whistling, peeping, screeching and crying. These songs you would notice well enough when you take an evening or early morning walk in the quiet areas of your locality. You would also notice the way it washes through your soul with peace and joy. Talk more of the joy it would give you when these joy givers are just by your window.

7. Birds make a great pet. They have feelings just like mammals and tend to express them in the sounds they make; this you can discover when you study their sounds. For instance, the owl lets out a loud cry in the night to alert danger. Other birds also cry when something sad happens to them. Hence, they are very easy to relate with. It is very wonderful to have a creature that you can relate t its feelings, have a chat with or play with. Some birds, when trained well, can communicate with humans, not necessarily through words but sounds. You would have to study them to discover what each sound they make implies, but if you ask me, I'll tell you that is even what makes it more interesting. If you are looking for a great pet, then don't look too far; you can find one in a bird.

Now, you might be wondering what a good birdhouse, in particular, has for the environment. Having a birdhouse could help you achieve pollination, weed control, amongst other things because for you to have birds very close by, it helps you improve the eco system and keep the garden tidy. And the only way to get them to visit constantly is by building a birdhouse that will act as a dwelling place and also attract them to keep coming around. Any structure that encourages or aids the existence of birds is largely beneficial to the general society. Birdhouses usually come in different fashion and designs to suit the ambiance, bird type, or environment.

1. Birdhouse provides a place that helps birds achieve successful reproduction. It allows them to raise their young until they are strong and grown. The environment is not safe for the birds to lay their eggs just anywhere. Hence, the birdhouse provides them with a place to safely lay their eggs and breed them until it hatches at maturity without being crushed. Even after the young birds grow, they have a place to lay their head until they decide to part. This helps to keep the cycle of evolution in order.

2. Also, it keeps them safe from disruptions in the environment. Just like you need shelter to hide you from disasters like war or natural disasters, birds also need that safe place where

they can hide from these disruptions, escape harm and have guaranteed security.

3. The birdhouse helps them to have a balanced and relaxed system of life. Hence they are more productive and happier. It is just like when you have a comfortable place to stay; your productivity is multiplied.

4. Birdhouses usually come with holes that allow the bird to have free entry and exit. When birds fly out through the holes, they tend to start working on the soil. As they do so, they etch the soil with their claws while walking. This singular action makes the soil loose and absorbent. This etch creates something like topsoil with various nutrients; this increases good bacteria and gives a good pH balance. Their feces also serve as a good compost for fertilizer. Hence, adding more strength and quality to the soil.

5. The birdhouse also allows you to keep different species of birds at the same time in one place. It is much easier to manage a

conservation center today using the birdhouses. You can create a quarter of birdhouses, where you house different species of friendly birds.

6. The birdhouse can be sold. If you have some bird lover friends or know any animal reserve center, you can be contacted to make different birdhouse sizes for them. This is a business opportunity you have to take advantage of. You do have a lot to gain and very little to lose.

Chapter 2

Birdhouse Construction Basics

Building a birdhouse isn't technical, at least not as technical as building a house. If you have considered building a birdhouse, it is because you have some love for these creatures and you want to ensure they are safe. However, loving them is not enough to guarantee their safety; you have to be able to build a place for them.

As much as you want to build a birdhouse, there are still some basics you need to know if you will get it right. You have to be equipped with the right knowledge to build a good and standard birdhouse. But you still have to consider the purpose of building a birdhouse, as this will affect the model and pattern or design of the birdhouse.

Different models are used in building birdhouses. It is all dependent on the intended use of the birdhouse. Birdhouses are usually built for exterior and interior uses; most specifically, some birdhouses are built for exhibition. You cannot compare the type of birdhouse built for interior use with the ones made for exhibition or used in reserves or conservation centers.

However, I can picture you already have an imaginary idea of the kind of birdhouse that you want for yourself. So, you are more interested in the details you need to get, the requirements or resources you need to garner, or the steps you need to take to achieve a birdhouse just like the image you have in your head.

The birdhouse selection criteria don't permit you to choose at random because you like a particular birdhouse color or model. Remember, it is not just about you. There are some specific details you need to take into consideration. I have already talked about the fact that you need to consider the location where the birdhouse will be placed and the need for the birdhouse. Well, we know the birdhouse is built to house birds, but for what reason in particular? To host them as pets inside the house, have them at the yard as a neighbor, or train them for sale or exhibitions.

You have to define this because every birdhouse type has its own specific requirement. And we are not just talking about colors; there are basic things that you have to consider. In this chapter, we will be talking about these requirements; some of them has been listed below;

1. Species of birds: This is not really a crucial point but one factor you have to consider. Most birds do not really have a preference for where they would love to be sheltered. If you pay attention to the way most birds structure their nest, you'll notice some slight differences, and one of them is space. We will be talking about that below. However, you have to be informed on how cavity nesters build their nest inside the birdhouse.

2. Size/shape of the birdhouse: The size of the birdhouse to a very large extent determines how comfortable the bird will be. Most people have the ideology that bigger is always better, but that's not true in itself. Excess space is bad as not having enough space, so you have to ensure that the size of your birdhouse is just right and suitable for the species of bird you plan to host. Birds are just like every other animal, and they have their terrestrial and adaptive behavior. They nest, reproduce, breed, move about and they require enough space to do so. Also, you have to ensure that the birdhouse is not just large in size but is tough enough to absorb the weight of the

bird. The right birdhouse for you doesn't need to be too big or too small; it should be compact enough to contain the number of birds you want it to accommodate, give it space to move freely about, reproduce and breed. But space should still be moderate.

3. Style of birdhouse's hole: At this point, I would have to remind you again that the birdhouse modifications are all about the bird and not about you. You know, if you are not conscious of this, you might get lost in the whole Magwire and begin to design the birdhouse to your taste. The birdhouse should only be designed to the bird's taste, not yours. This is why you must have an idea of the species of bird you are designing for. It will guide you to know what you would add and what you won't. Talking about the birdhouse hole, there are different sizes for different species of bird. This doesn't mean that you must measure the hole at exactly the diameter that the bird is looking for before you get it right. Just ensure to find a size that is as close as possible to the diameter you are looking for. It is only important

so that you can achieve accuracy. However, in general, the hole must be small. Also, hole size is key because it discourages unwanted birds from accessing the birdhouse; if not, any Peter and Paul would be living in the birdhouse. Finally, on this subject, endeavor to place a roof over the entrance hole to prevent rain and blizzards from disturbing the peace of your birds.

4. Birdhouse doors: Inasmuch as a birdhouse is generally viewed as a house of birds., humans still require access to the birdhouse. You need to clean the birdhouse when the birds are done breeding; they will definitely defecate and mess up the place. How would you clean it up if you don't have access to the interiors? Don't think of the hole. It is too tiny to contain your two fingers, talk more of allowing you clean and tidy up the interior. For this cause, it is required that you build a door, make one of the sides an access door for you to be able to clean the inside well. To build the door, you would need to use hinges on one of the sides. Some other persons use screws or not and bolt. So, when they want to open it,

which is once in a long while, they unbolt the sides and clean up the place, then bolt it back without much hassles. So, it is not out of place to say that the birdhouse door is as important as the hole. Also, the birdhouse door can be located at any side, the front, back, bottom, top, left or right sides. There is no specific place it must be placed, unlike the hole, which must specifically be in the front.

5. Material used in building: Birdhouses can be made of any material. However, the most common material used in birdhouse building is wood. Right from the time when birdhouses were invented, the material used in building was wood from trees. And they were different building plans that can be made using wood. The use of other materials like plastic, metals, concrete, and others came much later. Although, these materials are also very good and durable in themselves. However, the most trusted, acceptable, safest, and easiest-to-use type of material in building a birdhouse is wood. There are other supportive materials used in building;

they will be talked about in one of the coming chapters. We will also get to fully discuss the type of wood that is used in building for specific purposes.

6. Birdhouse roof: This is another essential that must be considered when building a birdhouse. The roof serves three main purposes; it prevents water from leaking into the birdhouse. It protects the bird from harsh weather conditions like sun and cold. It also acts as a protective structure from predators. Finally, the roof mobilizes water efficiently and prevents it from draining the nest. To achieve this, the roof needs to meet specific features. Some of them will be discussed here, and others will be discussed in the coming chapters. Firstly, the roof must be tilted or slant. This will channel the water or rain to trickle through one particular direction and reduce its chances of draining the inside of the birdhouse. The second feature is that it must cover the birdhouse fully. The roof must stretch out and cover up to the hole of the birdhouse to prevent the rain from trickling into the birdhouse. The

roof must also extend beyond the birdhouse. To avoid water leakages, the roof must be made of waterproof materials. For this sake, you can decide to add an aluminon or tin bar to the top surface. There is a downside to using this material, metal is a conductor of heat, so it could increase the heat of the birdhouse. Adversely, it could make the birds uncomfortable.

7. Birdhouse roof and interior designs: The inside of the birdhouse is just as important as the outside. Some builders usually neglect this part of the birdhouse, and they end up making a mistake that could endanger the bird. The interior of the birdhouse has to be safe and comfortable before it could be called perfect. One common mistake among builders is to use extra-long nails. The tip of the nail gets to stretch out beyond the wood into the birdhouse, and this is very dangerous. It could hamper the life of the bird or the chicks. Eventually, they would have to leave the birdhouse because the nails made it discomforting. Again, you would need to consider the nature of the species of bird you

intend to host when designing the interior. Birds like pigeons would require a rough interior where they can conveniently build their own nest. When building, leave the floor fairly rough. Design the interior carefully and strategically such that there should be a little ladder or milestone under the exit hole that would be used as an escape by the bird in time of danger. You could build an escape ladder by adding a piece of cloth strip into the house. First of all, make a good number of tiny holes in the cloth, hang it from the birdhouse's hole to the inside of the birdhouse, and the escape ladder is set. Aside from escaping from predators, this ladder would also be useful to chicks learning to fly. It grants them easy access and exit out of the birdhouse. It makes climbing easy.

8. Birdhouse perches or other designs: Birdhouse perches are that little stick or rod sticking out of the birdhouse in the front side of the house, just below the bird hole. Birds love perches, especially small birds. They love to sit on it in the cool of the day and navigate the surroundings. Studies also

show that birdhouses with perches attract more guests, as it is an enticing factor. However, there is a debate arguing if birdhouses with perches are good. You might be surprised and wondering why such a debate would arise in the very first instance. The actual truth is that these perches are usually located on the outside of the birdhouse and are very much exposed to danger. Ye, it is a very good idea to have one in your birdhouse, some expert bird watchers recommend it as they state it makes the bird feel more relaxed and comfortable, and I must add that it also makes the birdhouse appear beautiful. However, as we consider comfort and coziness when building the birdhouse, we must also consider the safety of the animals. Hangers aren't safe for birds as it exposes them to their predators; they become a clean catch. Twitchell also truthfully pointed out that birds do not really need the perches in their birdhouse; she states that it serves more aesthetic than practical purposes. Well, this is not to discourage you from having one if you desire to build one. You can add perches for smaller birds.

However, it is much more dangerous for bigger birds as they have bigger holes.

9. Drainage and ventilation system: Birdhouses, you must remember, are often outdoors. Irrespective of the number of measures taken, water will still find its way in. However, what you must ensure is being able to get rid of the water safely. To this end, it is suggested that an opening of at least four small holes be made in the floor of the birdhouse. This will help prevent the accumulation of water.

   Ventilation in birdhouses is also a requisite necessity. It is recommended that two holes at least are made to prevent internal overheating. These holes should be made either in the front or sidewalls of the birdhouse, specifically at the height of the entrance and exit holes of the bird.

However, you also need to know that all of these basics don't nullify your own ideas and birdhouse plans. You could still design that birdhouse of your dreams by using this list here as a guideline. Remember, it doesn't have to appear impressive.

It just has to be convenient enough to serve its purpose.

Here is a list to guide you in understanding the sizes of entrance holes for respective birds that are common.

Bird type	Floor size	Floor height	Entrance hole size	Entrance hole height	Mounting height
Wren	4×4, 6×6	7-8 inch	1 inch	5-6 inch	5-10 feet
Chickadee	4×4	9	1-1/8	7	5-15 feet
Nuthatch	4×4	8-9	1-3/8	7	5-20 feet
House Finch	5×5	8	1-1/2	7	5-10
Eastern bluebird	5×5	10	1-1/2	8	4-6
Tree swallow	5×5	6-8	1-1/4	5-6	5-15
Woodpecker	4×4	9	1-3/8	7	5-20
Northern Flicker	7×7	17	2-1/2	15	10-15
Kestrel	8×8	12-16	3	9-13	10-30
Owl	8×8	16	3	13	10-30
Wood duck	12×12	22	4	17	15
Purple Martin	6×6	6-8	1-3/4	1-2	10-20
Violet green swallow	5×5	6-8	1-1/4	4-6	5-15
Warbler	5×5	6-8	1-1/2	4-6	15-30

Chapter 3

Bird House Building Tips

1. Ensure that the small chicks or younger birds will be able to climb out of the birdhouse. Roughen the inside of the birdhouse, just below the exit hole. You can also attach a galvanized wire mesh of ¼-inch so the young can easily climb out of the birdhouse.

2. Wood is the best material to use in building birdhouses because it's flexible and more durable. However, not all woods can be used in woodworking for birdhouses. Avoid treated woods and woods as fragile as plywood.

3. You would need to provide nesting materials for birds like the woodpeckers, waterfowl, and owls with nesting material. The cavity-nesting birds can build their own nest by carrying twigs and pieces of wood to build, but it is not the same with the woodpeckers. You would need to

provide materials for them to build with, or they might struggle with building their own nest.

4. Seal your fasteners: Screwing during the assembling of the birdhouse is a good and quicker option to nailing. Asides screw, another very good fastener is the ring-shank nails. These are the better types of fasteners that you should use. Using the conventional fasteners will make the joints loose, especially if you are using wood like cedar or redwood because they have thick textures. You can use this fastener on the pinewood. Don't assemble with glue alone; endeavor to use the right fasteners depending on your wood type. Although beginning the assemble with glue makes it stronger.

5. To attract birds to your birdhouse, you can place nest-building materials inside the house; you could also place feathers, feeders, yarn, strings, amongst other things that should be neatly kept inside the birdhouse. This is not necessary or compulsory in itself, but it is a tip that could make your visiting bird stay longer. Not all birds

use nesting materials; birds that don't use nesting materials should have their birdhouse littered about with a layer of sawdust or round cork.

6. Aside from building an entrance hole or access into the birdhouse, to encourage the birds to move about freely, you have to make the inside rough to have a firm grip on the ground and have ease while exiting or entering. Not all birds will be comfortable with a clean and smooth slope. Many experts suggest that using a rough sawn wood would make it easier for the birds to be more comfortable.

7. Secure your floor: Ensure that the sides of the wood are in a direct enclosure with the floor. You can use screws or nails to make it firmly secured. This will protect the inside from rain.

8. Do not keep your birdhouse too high for easy maintenance, so you can comfortably reach out and clean or monitor the birdhouse without having to shift it or unhang it.

9. Shield the surrounding of the birdhouse: Make sure to attach the birdhouse to a fixed position, then create an iron or metal shield to the post or tree holding the birdhouse to discourage predators from launching an attack. Also, grease the post, and you can leave wren houses suspended in the air.

10. Use coatings with caution: Do not try coating the interior of the birdhouse; no bird would stay there. Ensure to use only paints that are made with natural elements to coat the exterior of the birdhouse. The interior shouldn't be coated. Be careful about the colors you use in coloring the outside. Colorful or too brightly adorned birdhouses will Purple martins prefer their houses stay white but together cavity nesters prefer grey and any other color.

11. A birdhouse with good ventilation is very comfortable for nesting birds, without the exposure to harsh weather conditions like heat, cold or rainy leaks. Make holes of 5/8" diameter on either side at the top to cause air circulation

and prevent the house from getting suffocated. If you happened to have built your birdhouse without ventilation holes, you could still drill those little holes in the top side of the building.

12. Place the house in a location where it is not in direct relationship with sunlight. If it is placed in a shade, it helps keep the house cool than directly facing the heat.

13. You can use metal guards to protect the birdhouse from predators, even though you are not allowed to build with metals.

14. Make holes of 3/8" in diameter at the bottom or floor of the birdhouse.

15. Place the birdhouse carefully. We will still talk extensively on birdhouse placing, but you just need to be conscious of the distance between the birdhouse and the ground for the fundamental knowledge. Ensure the box is placed at a perfect height from the ground. Placing it at the wrong height, or too close to the ground might expose it to predators and subject it to attack. Also, taking

it too high might make the birds feel uncomfortable. Hence, you must find an even height to place the birdhouse. The location you place the birdhouse is very important to be considered. The surface must be smooth and sturdy. The birdhouse shouldn't be shaky or swinging. Whatever surface you choose, pole, fence, or rooftop, endeavor to confirm its safety and sturdiness. The entrance hole should be positioned to face another angle other than any windy or breezy direction. Most importantly, ensure that the location of the birdhouse is sturdy and highly positioned in a very safe place.

16. Don't overcrowd one area with many birdhouses: As beautiful as having more than one birdhouse in a location might appear, it could also be very dangerous, as it attracts more and dangerous predators for a juicy feast. Another point to consider is that some birds do not tolerate close neighbors. Birds like the cavity nesters appreciate their space and always want to be in charge of their territory. Imagine putting two-cavity nesters birdhouses together in one place; it is definitely

going to be a catastrophe. Although, birds like Sparrows are much different and very accommodating. They can even nest in a neighboring nest without problems, but this is not so for all birds. Hence, the basic distance for each birdhouse should be 50 feet or apart. So, it is best for you to create your birdhouses in quite distant locations, far apart from each other.

17. Construct your birdhouse in a way that you can still gain full access every time and anytime. Build a door or accessible roof that can easily remove so you can gain access to the inside of the birdhouse and clean it or make modifications.

18. Consistently clean and maintain the birdhouse: This is not only pertaining to the interiors of the nest box even though it seems it is the main place to be cleaned. It is no news that birds drop droppings of feces in their nest boxes. These droppings could be massively discomforting for the bird. It could breed insects and harmful creatures, which can hamper the health of the chicks. An unclean environment is not safe for

anyone, so do well to clean out the birdhouse of your birds every once in a while and maintain that healthy lifestyle. You would see that your birds would grow naturally.

19. Build a house for a specific bird: It is very important that a birdhouse is created for a particular bird. Create a birdhouse for a cavity-nesting bird that lives in your region.

20. Provide adequate ventilation: Ensure that your birdhouse is well ventilated. Drill tiny holes through each side of the birdhouse; this will provide proper air circulation.

21. Do not add perches for big birds: Perches expose the birds to harmful predators like Jays, Magpies, Ravens, and Crows. It could give the predatory birds wrong access to the birds in the nest box. The cavity-nesting birds do not consistently use perches; they prefer birdhouses without perches. If indeed you finally resolve to build the perches, you have to make sure it is safe enough for you.

22. Build a box that will stay dry and warm: Place the roof of the birdhouse strategically so that it successfully sustains and keeps the birdhouse warm. Also, ensure that the box is well screwed and tight.

23. Building a birdhouse is much easier if you have the plans and drawn-out designs.

24. To give a professional touch or result, use only the right tools and materials.

25. Do not use the wrong instrument to stand in for the right one; it has to be right for it to appear professional.

Tips for Birdhouse Design and Building

Building a birdhouse might appear easy, well that's if all you seek to produce is a wooden box with an entrance hole. A good and standard birdhouse is a creative work and requires great time and effort to make it a reality. You also need a good bank of knowledge to make productive efforts, and that's what this chapter is all about; to educate you on all you need to know about birdhouse building. Even though you have years of experience in woodworking, you'd still need to learn the nitrites of making an attractive and bird-friendly birdhouse.

Think of what attracts birds to a house: I know you're quite excited about this birdhouse building, but you know you're not going to live in it. You're making it for a bird. So, how do you attract the bird to its house, or better put the house you built for it? That's quite an important subject to brood upon. Well, you don't have to think so much, just the way we humans look for some specific features when we want to buy a house, the same way it is with animals. You can go ahead to list those search points that you look for when buying a house: a large kitchen, enough bedroom space, good ventilation, amongst others. There are a few factors that birds are very conscious of when they are selecting a birdhouse or a nesting place.

Entrance hole size: This has been emphasized enough. The size of the hole is one great thing to consider when you build. No bird will want to squeeze into a hole that's not accommodating. The bird hole determines the kind of birds that would stay in your birdhouse. Chapter two has the list of sizes of entrance holes for each bird.

Asides from the entrance hole, you have to measure the right overall cavity depth and height. The height or distance from the ground is necessary to be considered.

The interior floor dimensions should be determined and will be measured using the bottom side of the wood.

General house shape and design should be designed in a way that the birds would be attracted easily.

There are several house location options and mounting styles to be considered. Make sure to select the one that your bird most prefers. When you position the birdhouse in the right place, you tend to attract more birds permanently. They wouldn't just visit one-time, but they would want to visit time and time again.

A birdhouse isn't complicated or complex in itself, so you don't have to make complex plans before you can get it right. If it is your first time building a birdhouse, it is only wise that you put aside your invention and start with a tried-and-true plan. There are 15 of them listed in this book. Ensure to follow them step by step. Each design or style you see is very flexible; you can change it and create your own patterns, but following already outlaid patterns helps you to understand the basics easily. Afterward, you can confidently make your own designs and teach others to do the same.

A Short message from the Author:

Hey, I hope you are enjoying the book? I would love to hear your thoughts!

Many readers do not know how hard reviews are to come by and how much they help an author.

```
Customer Reviews
★★★★★ 2
5.0 out of 5 stars ▼
5 star  ████████ 100%    Share your thoughts with other customers
4 star             0%
3 star             0%    [ Write a customer review ]  ⬅
2 star             0%
1 star             0%
See all verified purchase reviews ▸
```

I would be incredibly grateful if you could take just 60 seconds to write a short review on Amazon, even if it is a few sentences!

\>\> Click here to leave a quick review

Thanks for the time taken to share your thoughts!

Chapter 4

Getting Started with Birdhouse Buildings

Tools and Supplies

Building a sturdy, attractive, and weatherproof birdhouse requires that you use the right materials only. This is the only way it can be made possible.

Wood

Different types of woods can be used in birdhouse building, but not all of them eventually attract birds to the birdhouse. One major thing to consider when choosing a wood for building is its durability and ability to absorb texture or moisture. There are tens of wood in the world, but not all wood can be used in birdhouse building. It must be at least ¾" thick. Also, the woods must not be treated; fumes from the chemicals you used in treating the wood will stay residue on it and cause harm to the birds. There are mainly five types of woods used in building birdhouses, a list of them are;

- Cypress: The cypress is usually addressed as a wet climate wood. It has a unique wood texture that enables it to repel water. The cypress could however, deteriorate quickly if used with harsh elements like the sand. When it comes in direct contact with soil, it can begin to die or lose its texture. This shouldn't really be a problem since you are using it to build a birdhouse and you only have to be mindful of the location where you place it. This wood is very soft and allows you to put screws and nails quickly. You can freely leave the wood out in the open without finishing. To make it last longer, coat the outside with a natural varnish. Asides from this, cypress is a really great wood to use in making birdhouses.

- Redwood tree: The redwood was quite extinct many years back due to overlogging. However, as of present, it is being used again for woodworking projects. Just like the name implies, the redwood has an attractive red grain color. It exhumes a red pigment that is very compelling and attractive to behold. You don't have to worry about painting the birdhouse when you use this wood, as it exhumes a natural red pigment that is far from being toxic, unlike the artificial paints used in coating woods. Your birds are as good as saved. It is also very solid and durable. Using this wood won't just give your birdhouse exceptional strength, it will also give your birdhouse that strong and bold appearance. The redwood can easily scratch, but it doesn't affect the general appearance of birdhouses made with redwood. This wood is a perfect choice for outdoor projects, and you need not worry about the effect of water on this wood. It has a strong natural resistance to weather.

- Pine: This is one of the commonest woods used in making woodworking projects. It is very easy to get irrespective of the location where you base, you could always find a pine wood, because it is very available, it is the cheapest of all woods that will be listed here. Looking for a cost-effective wood to use in your woodworking project that wood is the pine wood. The pine wood is nature's gift to man, it is very easy to cut through, and work with, because it is soft. It has a very fine grain that doesn't require finishes to make it look appealing. It is not too water resistant. It is best used in heat period. It doesn't shrink or swell in hot temperature. it has the ability to withstand heat waves. Feel free to throw the colors on as pine perfectly absorbs paint.

- Teak wood: This is a new wood type that has almost the same feature as the cypress wood. It produces natural oil that acts as a repellant for water. This oil also chases away rot, decay, and insects. You don't have to burden the wood to make it last longer. On its own, it can last for several years without modification under any weather; rain or sunshine. This is the best wood for birdhouse building.

- Oakwood: The oakwood naturally stands out as it is very hard and provides this form of rigidity and stamina that is rare amongst other woods. With this wood, you don't need to use chemical-based paints or vanishes. The oak has a very attractive and natural look ranging from swirling patterns to tiger-striped with yellow flecks.

- Cedar: This wood is great as it produces moisture that repels insects. It lasts as long as other woods and more. If it is left in the open sun and rain for days, it will certainly not rot badly. This wood is strong enough to last in the open for 10 to 15 years without stress. This wood type also has a very attractive appearance that seeks to draw attention. It is also very much expensive. It offers a unique form of insulation that enables the birds to stay warm even in winter. Unlike other tough woods, this wood doesn't swell or shrink when it rains. It best withstands insect damages than other woods.

Fasteners and Glue

Fasteners and glues are usually used together in assembling all the sides of the birdhouse after woodworking. Many builders first apply the glue before attaching the fastener. This isn't a rule, but using them together helps you give your birdhouse some firmness and rigidity. Gluing before fastening would help extend the life and strength of the birdhouse. The normal fasteners that are used are the brass shrank nails, hinges, and screws. These types of fasteners are more rust-resistant and hold more firmly and tightly. Of all the fasteners, nails are easier to use; they also last longer when they are made of steel. You can decide to use only the nail throughout the birdhouse. If using a finishing nail, it should be about 1-1/4" in length. The distance between the roof and the sides should be minimal to create an overhanging roof, nail ¾" from the edge of the roof. Screws are better fasteners to use because they hold sturdier last longer and are flexible. You can easily unscrew a particular screw when that part of the birdhouse has a problem. Common glues used in birdhouse buildings are the wetproof glue that won't be affected by rain or water. Some of these glues have really harsh chemicals, so you should be careful as you apply them. When using the hinges or any other fastener, be careful to prevent the sharp edges from sticking into the interior of the birdhouse. It poses a great danger to the bird.

Handsaw

The handsaw is very necessary as it is used in cutting down aggregate measurements of the wood pieces. The handsaw is very precise and cuts very accurately. The handsaw enables you to make the rough shown in the wood as you cut to enable the bird to hold a firm group on the wood.

Chisel

There are different types and forms of chisel. However, the basic chisel has a wooden handle and a thick metal blade with a sharpened edge. The chisel is used to make cuts of specific that is used by driving it with a hammer or mallet. It is mainly used in cutting out the shape of the entrance hole.

Hand-Powered Drill

Some of these drills have been replaced by power drills. The hand drill is used today by just a few woodworkers today. The hand drill is made of a cranking handle that is used to turn pinion gears on the main shaft. There is a drill bit at the end of the shaft. It is used to drill holes in wood. To make the drill, pressure is applied to the top part and the grip is used to rotate the tool.

Drill or Driver

It is used in drilling really big holes; the final connection is sunk into the wood so the drill can drive through it and make exclusively large holes. This is also used in driving fasteners into the wood. It sometimes needs the input of the hammer to have a successful drive into the wood. Drills generally vary in size, speed and power.

Drill Bits

It is used to drill a small hole in the wood for nails or screws so that the wood doesn't break or scatter under the influence of the nail. It is majorly used for predrilling holes. This is the part of the drill that makes the hole.

Jigsaw

It is used in making circular cuts around the side of the wood. It is used specifically to make unique and intricate cuts. It has a narrow blade that is attached to the main tool's body from a spring-loaded clamp positioned in front. It is safe to use and makes very accurate cuts.

Hole Saw Set

This is a box of different sizes of hole saws. Hole saw comes in different diameters to cut the hole, i.e., when you want to drill large holes. The hole saw is a cylinder made from steel with saw teeth to cut into the top edge. It creates a hole in the workplace without having to cut up the material. It is usually used in a drill. They are used to cut perfectly round holes in materials.

Hammer

You don't need that big hammer; you are working on a simple birdhouse, so the hammer needed is the finishing hammer. It is lighter than the normal hammer and adds just the right pressure to the wood.

Tape Measure

This is very important as it enables the builder to measure the wood properly before he makes the cut. In birdhouse building, you don't just speculate the point of cutting with your eyes, you have to run the measurement, and the way to make the measurement is by using the tape measure. You can choose to use a metal tape measure.

Clamps

The clamp is used in holding the work together while sawing and after gluing or fastening so that the attachment is safe and sturdy.

T-Square

The T-square, also known as farmer's square, is used in marking straight lines before cutting. It is a large ruler used in making angles and straight lines. It is very essential when you want to make straight cuts.

Screwdriver

If you used screws in place of nails or hinges, you would understand its use, as this is the only scenario where the screwdriver is useful in birdhouse building. You can use it to screw or unscrew your screws.

Keeping Birdhouse Safe From Predators

The season of nesting is always hazardous for birds, as they get more exposed to dangers and predators attack. Because the birds are always less mobile, they spend time in their nest sitting over their young ones until it hatches. They spend a lot of time in the nest than they do outside. The predators usually know this, so they strike in such time, wanting to hunt and eat their birds and chicks. If, for any reason, the birdhouse is not well protected against this attack, it is already in danger.

Most predators hunt specifically for young chicks; they usually find it very interesting and delicious than the adult bird. Hence, in as much as the adult bird might be big enough to defend itself, its young one is still susceptible to attacks. Therefore, you must protect the birdhouse from hungry predators. Some of the predators of birds are; cats, snakes, Raccoons, Squirrels, rats, mice, bears, chipmunks, and opossums.

The most common ones are cats, snakes and mice. This is because they are majorly found around the domestic areas where these birds are also located. These are animals you must beware of, and once you ignore their existence and leave the birdhouse unguarded, you are exposing the birds to serious danger.

Asides from these animals that have been mentioned here, it was discovered that larger birds could also be predators. This is the way it is in the animal world. The largest intimidates the smallest and seeks to take advantage of them if not even rob them. Birds that commonly cause problems like this are the Jays, Crows, Startling, Magpies and other large birds that are apivorous in nature. Most times, they just come snatch the eggs and take advantage of eggs and chicks as an easy food source once they obtain into the birdhouse.

It is very important that you decipher the type of danger that the birdhouse is exposed to; this will help you plan and prepare a proper guard to save your bird from that particular type of danger. Birds on rooftops are exposed to predators like cats or mice or larger birds.

One way to control predators attack is by placing your birdhouse in safe and perfect positions. For birdhouses that are placed on trees, they are mostly exposed to predators like snake.

There are some techniques you needed to practice that will help you protect your birdhouse effectively:

Hole restrictors: It is not enough that the hole is small and tiny. No matter how tiny you make the hole, some predators will still go ahead to eat up the wood around the hole so that they can enlarge it wide enough for their entry. The hole restrictor is a metal fastened around the hole to prevent enlargement and unsolicited entry. The hole restrictor would permit only birds of appropriate sizes to enter. Here is another reason you must make actual measurements of the bird's required hole size before you commence cutting. This is a life saver, as it helps to secure a large percentage of the bird folk. So, you have a huge homework to do; ensure to ascertain the required hole size for every type of bird you want.

Tube entrance: This is achieved by using an elongated tube placed inside the birdhouse. What this does is that it makes the entrance long. The bird would have to pass through the tunnel before they enter the birdhouse. Like the cavity nesters, most birds don't really mind the extension, but it turns off the predators. They won't be able to pass through such a thin hole.

Most predators cannot make the extra reach and stretch through the long tube to capture any of the birds inside. You can place a simple piece of pipe 1-3 inches long in the hole to achieve this. If you would be doing this, ensure to give more space in your birdhouse, as you would need a lot of extra space for the bird to move around. If properly done, it could appear aesthetic and like a camouflage. The tube entrance should not be so long, so it wouldn't frustrate or encourage the birds for which it was made. Also, it shouldn't be so short that it wouldn't encourage the predator's visit.

Roof size: Predators rarely attack from the roof. Most large predators like the Raccoons, Squirrels, and Cats usually sit on the birdhouse roof, irrespective of where it is located, and stretch inside to attack the bird and chicks. This usually occurs when the roof is quite small and spreads unevenly, this is why the roof must be large enough to secure the hole. The roof must be made longer, such that the front extends by 5-6 inches, and the sides 2-3 inches. This creates a built-in battle to prevent the predator from getting its hands into the hole and on the chick.

Remove perches: We have talked a lot about perches and now you would agree with me that it actually does more harm than good. Without the perch, the bird can still access the house conveniently; it could decide to stand on some tree branch if it doesn't want to sit in the birdhouse. The perch provides a good handhold for predators and grants them unprecedented access to the chick. It is a good platform for the predator to gain entry into the hole. Also, remove any tree branch close to the birdhouse.

Train outdoor pets to stay away from birdhouses: If you can train your pets to answer their name, you can condition their behavior to what you want or how you like it to be. This is termed behavioral conditioning. There are so many methods of behavioral conditioning that can be used. One effective method is using the water hose to chase the dog away anytime they try coming close to the birdhouse. Once you do this repeatedly, the pet will consciously start to avoid the birdhouse. To use any behavioral condition, you need patience and perseverance. Also, ensure that pets are supervised when they are outdoors, especially during the nesting season. Young birds are most likely to fall prey because they usually move outside their nest for days before They start flying. Your attention needs to be upon all of them.

Use the right hole size for the birdhouse opening: If the birdhouses have a poor hole size, it will attract predators and grant them smooth and stress-free access into the birdhouse. So, ensure your birdhouse has the right hole size.

Position the birdhouse a distance away from the bush: Some predators could be hiding under the green grass even though you want to locate it close to the plants to allow birds to scout the arena. Also, make sure there is a good distance between birdhouses and feeding areas. A distance of eight feet is good enough.

Choose natural colors so the birdhouse will blend with the color of the surrounding, the color of nature. Dark green and brown are good choices that are well attractive to birds. Decorate the exterior of the house with natural tools to keep it from being too obvious.

Predator Guards and Its Importance

There are several predator guards built in the birdhouse. A few of them are listed below;

- Bird-eye predator guard: This is a round plastic that is placed above the entry hole of the birdhouse. It installs very easily over the entry hole. It has a lock that you can use to secure your nest box. You can choose to install or uninstall it. It has a 2.25" depth and 1.5" diameter that helps prevent predators from gaining access to the inside of the birdhouse.

- Metal baffles: You can add a predator guard by adding metal baffles both above and below the house. They make it difficult to climb when the birdhouse is placed on top of a single and slim pillow.

- Stovepipe battle: This device is made from a stovepipe and it encircles the position between the hardware cloths and straps

- Noel predator guard: This has the shape of a rectangle tube of clothes glued or stapled to the birdhouse's front side. This will help make it difficult for the predators to gain access into the box while the birds maintain free transport.

- Conical metal predator guard: This guard is usually attached to a free-standing pole. This guard is made from a circular piece of metal attached with a pole placed directly under the box.

Importance of predator guards

- It stops the predators from reaching the birdhouse
- It also improves nesting success for the birds, as they would have run away if they feel threatened.
- It encourages more visits from different species of birds.

Placement of Birdhouse

Placing your birdhouse in the right position is very important. Failure to fully understand where a birdhouse should be placed could make it as good as useless and expose it to danger.

Good repositioning makes your birdhouse attractive and appealing to the birds. No matter your design on the birdhouse or how beautiful you must have made it, it only makes good sense when mounted in the right place.

Here is a list of general considerations you should make that should guide your selection of a birdhouse:

- The entrance hole should be positioned to face the opposite direction of a prevailing wind. This

is to prevent sunshine and rain from directly reflecting or entering the birdhouse.
- Do not place the birdhouse close to birdfeeders to prevent intimidation from bigger birds or attack from predators.
- Birds use birdhouses that are in a location they love. If no bird happens to have visited your birdhouse after a while, then it is possible it is not in a comfortable place; you might have to change location.

Below are places you can mount your birdhouse, possible locations to consider;

- A pole: Many builders love placing their birdhouse here, as it is far away from the ground and discourages many predators from climbing up to it. The size and height are two major discouraging factors. If it is a metal pole, it is more difficult for predators to climb. However, you can't just place your birdhouse on the pole, it is going to crash over your head. You need a mounting bracket. There are many of them that make it easy to install the birdhouse on a metal pipe, a wooden post, or a metal t-post.

- Tree trunks: Birds naturally live on trees, so this idea is very welcoming. Tree trunks are very stable bases on which birdhouses are installed. However, it is very accessible to predators as it is very easy for them to climb to the birdhouse. Therefore, ensure that the bird hole is very small to prevent predators like squirrels from gaining access to the eggs or young birds.

- Hang from tree: Materials used in hanging birdhouses are wire, rope, or chain. It is also a safe option and unreachable by predators. Remember that birds won't stay in a swaying birdhouse. Therefore you have to keep the rope short, so the birdhouse can be very stable.

- Slippery building façade: This is a good location as it also discourages predators from ascending the slippery slope up to the birdhouse. The only downside of this mounting position is that if the façade directly reflects the sun, the birdhouse will certainly overheat on sunny days.

Birdhouse mounting height

Here is a little guide for mounting birdhouse for common birds;

Bird species	Mounting height
Wren	6-10' (2-3m)
Tree swallow	5-10' (2-3m)
House sparrow	10-15' (3-5m)
Owl	10-15' (3-5m)
Purple Martin	10-15' (3-5m)
Nuthatches	10-15' (3-5m)
Woodpecker	10-20' (3-6m)
Warbler	5-10' (2-3m)
Bluebird	4-6' (1-2m)
House Finch	5-10' (2-3m)
Kestrel	10-20' (3-6m)
Chickadee	5-15' (2-5m)
Flicker	6-10' (2-3m)

Further note that not all birds prefer places out in the open like the bluebirds and purple martins. Ost birds prefer houses in camouflaged locations. They will have little impact from the sun and rain. Hence, they will last longer than usual.

Monitoring and Cleaning the Birdhouse

Most cavity nesters usually return at every nesting season to nest in the birdhouse; some of them, like the Eastern Phoebes, will not reuse a birdhouse if it is messy and untidy. Aside from encouraging the birds' return, you should clean out the birdhouse to also put away or prevent any form of disease through harmful bacteria and fungi. If the birdhouse is not cleaned, the bird might return and get infected and die. Also, when the birdhouse isn't cleaned up, residue nesting material gets piled up. The larger birds could come and take over the birdhouse and build with the nesting materials. Not cleaning the house makes the box more appealing to big birds like Critters.

Cleaning the birdhouse is a common courtesy you owe the birds if you really want them. It is just like cleaning up your guestroom after your guest has left.

Ensure to clean the birdhouse at least once a year, preferably after the nesting period. Some birds, like the bluebirds, have more than one nesting season. It is important that you clean it after every season.

Before you start cleaning, monitor and observe the activities to be sure that the birds are all departed, so you don't discard an active nest. Observe for a few days for signs of any happening activity. If there is none, visit the birdhouse and give it a gentle tap on the door. If you don't hear any chirping, it means the birdhouse is empty and ready to be evacuated.

Here are short steps as to how to clean the birdhouse

1. Get your cleaning tools; gloves, water, bucket, and bleach.
2. Bring down the birdhouse from the position you have placed it and open it up to clean the inside. The only way you can be able to open the birdhouse is if you had built a door. This is why you should never build your birdhouse without a door.
3. Now that you have gained access, put on your gloves, you are going to be taking everything out with your hands, and you sure wouldn't want to do that unprotected. Discard every single thing out of the birdhouse into a trash bag.

4. You might find some dried-up fecal matter, get a scraper and do justice to it by scrapping gently still wearing the rob.
5. Dilute your bleach in water
6. Use the water and probably a sponge because you stood your chance, give the birdhouse a good scrub, especially at all the corners and crevices.
7. Rinse the soapy water or bleach out using a hose.
8. Put the birdhouse under direct heat or sunlight to ensure it dries properly without growing mold or mildew.
9. It is inspection time; ensure that everything is the same and nothing is out of place.

Chapter 5

Birdhouse Plans and Ideas

At this point, you must have understood that your birdhouse plan doesn't have to impress anyone. It doesn't have to appear so attractive, colorful, or glamorous. Remember, you are not building for yourself, but animals who don't really have all the cares. So, there is no need to stress about colors and creative designs and all of those things. All you need is a comfortable place where your bird can dwell and be nested.

There are several birdhouse plans and ideas you could possibly try out; some are very much out of fashion and others are modern. Right here, I have made a compilation of 11 birdhouse plans you can build.

You would find them very simple and easy to make.

They are explained explicitly with step-by-step images that will guide you to achieving that great birdhouse.

Simple Birdhouse

This is a simple birdhouse plan you can make for the winter season, where most birds like the songbird are scouting to build their nests to stay warm throughout the season. As mentioned in the tips for building birdhouse plans, you should know that winter is one of the best times to put a birdhouse in your backyard if you intend to attract birds to your vicinity.

It is like setting a trap at the hole of the mouse hide; it has no choice but to step into it. The birds in wintertime are looking for a place to be shielded from the rain and the nest on the tree is not a very comfortable place for them. So, they would really appreciate your kind gestures if you put up this structure in the backyard or garden for them. Okay, not to dwell so much on this, let's list the materials used in building this.

Supplies

- Two pieces of hardwood, 1×6inch board and 1×8inch board
- Handsaw
- Screwdriver
- Drill

- Pen or pencil
- Hammer
- Measuring tape
- Straight edge
- Wood screws
- Finishing nails

Procedures

Step 1: Cut your top piece of wood to 10 inches by 8 inches. Then cut the 4-foot 1×6inch board. Begin by cutting the front and the sides before cutting the back. Make sure you use your measuring tape to confirm the measurements before you cut. Use the below image as a guideline for you to make your measurements and cut.

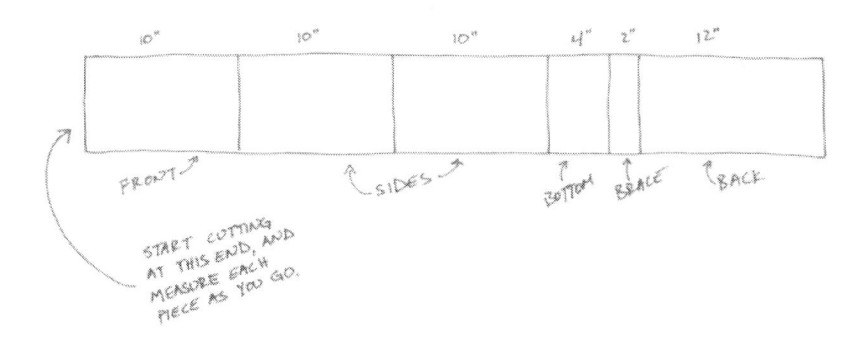

Step 2: Use a ¼ inch drill bit to drill a tiny hole at the corner of each corner of the bottom piece. This will serve as a drainage channel.

Step 3: Use a 1/8 inch drill bit to make screw holes in all the other pieces; front, back, and top pieces. Use the image below as your guide to how to make measurements before you cut.

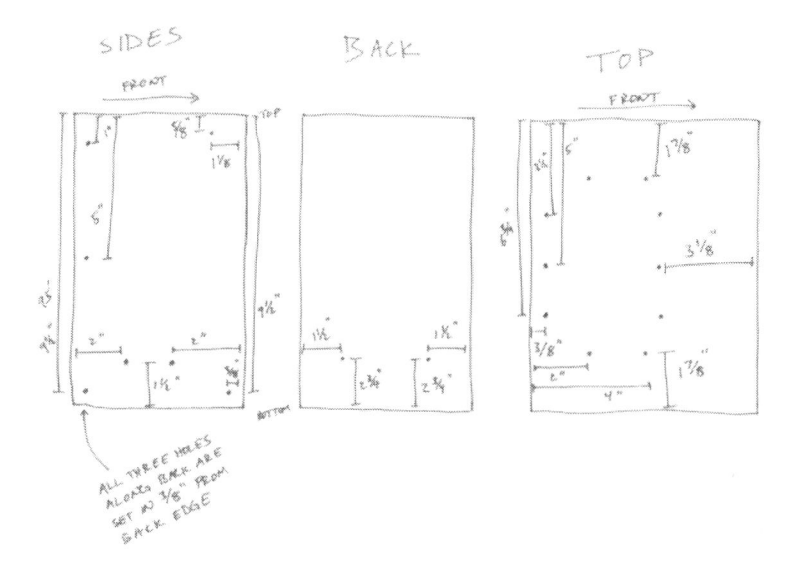

Step 4: Draw a line across the back piece on the inside part. The hole should be ½ inch from the top. Then use the hand saw to scratch off 4-6 inches in the center of the board. This is to make the surface quite rough, so it would be easy for the bird to climb in and out of it.

Step 5: Just before you assemble, make similar rough kerfs into the underside of the roof piece to create a drip line for the rain and prevent rain from being harsh and getting wicked into the box.

Step 6: Attach both sides to the box, using the front piece for support as you attach each side together.

Step 7: Attach the bottom to the backside by aligning it with the already drilled holes. Ensure that they all fit well without having to be forced.

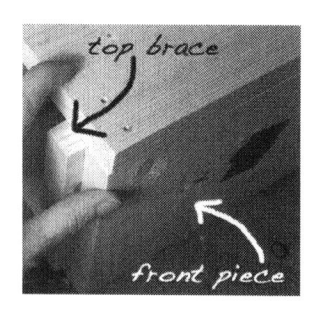

Step 8: Add the front brace and make sure it is fitted before adding the top piece to the box. There should be a small gap between the outer top of the box and the top of the front piece. You can block this gap by using the top brace. You would be using a nail to join the other pieces together, but you will use a screw on the front sides to easily unscrew when you want to look inside the box or clean it up. That will be your screw latch

Step 9: Mark the point in the front piece where you want to make your entrance hole. Drill at an angle that allows the entrance hole to slope slightly upward from outside to inside to prevent water from entering into the box when it rains.

Step 10: Sand the hole carefully to make it smooth. Be careful not to enlarge the hole while you sand it. Your birdhouse is ready!

Feel free to mount it to a tree, fence post, side of a building, tree trunk and any other structure.

Fence Picket Birdhouse

This birdhouse has been around for a long time. This is the conventional birdhouse that most people are familiar with. It is a project you can attempt to try out with your whole family together. There are very simple and direct steps you can follow to build this traditional birdhouse. They can be placed anywhere, but it is more of an interior birdhouse than the above birdhouse, which can be used only in the backyard or any exterior location. When assembling, children are to use glue while adults could use the nail.

Supplies

- Untreated cedar
- Handsaw
- Drill
- Measuring tape
- Nails
- Glue

Procedures

Step 1: Cut a 7 ¼" cut for the front and back sides. Cut the top corners off by making your 45-degree angle to achieve a house shape.

Step 2: Cut a 4 ¼ inch for the sidewalls, and cut an 8 ½" for the floor and roof pieces.

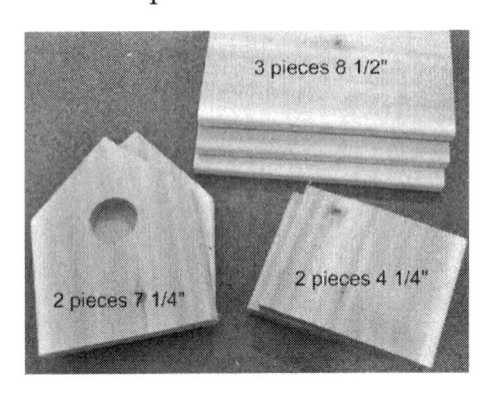

Step 3: Glue the floor to the back side to make them permanently attached together.

Step 4: Attach the side walls to the box.

Step 5: Make a 2" bit drill on the front pieces and attach it to the box.

Step 6: Attach the top to the box.

Modern Birdhouse

This is a modern and cheaper type of birdhouse. It allows you to economize your woods and make very simple cuts that could help you. Unlike the other types of birdhouse that doesn't really support painting, you can apply some paint stains to this birdhouse and make it appear more attractive.

You can also make this project with your children; the steps are children-friendly.

Supplies

- 1×6 hardwood (cedar)
- Circular saw
- Nails

Procedures

Step 1: Make a 5 ½" cut for the top and bottom pieces. Make a 5 ½ inch × 4 ¾ inch for the sides, and 5 ½ × 5inch for the front. Also, make a 5 ½ ×8 ½ inch for the backsides.

Step 2: It is time to attach all your pieces together. Before you start joining them together, ensure to drill the front hole for entry. For this project, you would be attaching the front pieces first before others. You would be attaching your front piece to the sides.

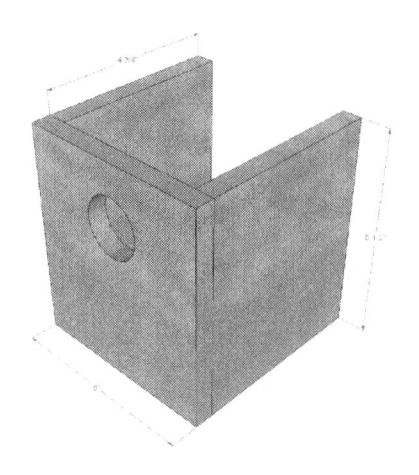

Step 3: Next, attach your top and bottom pieces.

Step 4: Finally, attach the back piece. If you are observant you would notice that it is longer than all other pieces. When attaching the back piece, make sure that it is well positioned such that the larger part of it is sticking out at the top.

Step 5: Go ahead to drill a hole in the back wood piece for hanging. Your birdhouse is ready.

Beginner Birdhouse

This project is exclusively for those new to the world of woodworking. You would learn how to cut accurately and assemble properly. This is also a traditional design. You can make all your cuts from a wood of 15 cm wide.

Supplies

- One 38 cm of cedar wood for the back

- Two 22×26 cm of cedar wood for the two side walls
- 18 cm of cedar wood for the roof
- 23 cm wood for the front side
- 1 base piece of 12 cm long.
- Wood glue
- Nails
- Screws
- Drills

Procedures

Step 1: Using the below-stated measurement and draw out the sizes on the plank, saw the plank according to those measurements

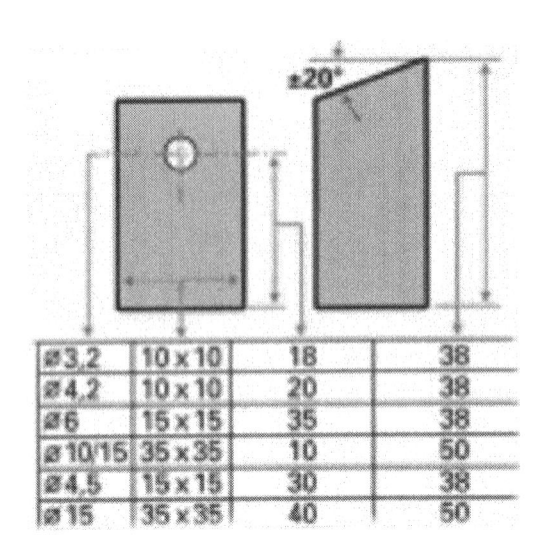

⌀3,2	10 x 10	18	38
⌀4,2	10 x 10	20	38
⌀6	15 x 15	35	38
⌀10/15	35 x 35	10	50
⌀4,5	15 x 15	30	38
⌀15	35 x 35	40	50

Step 2: Sand all the edges of the pieces lightly after cutting

Step 3: Drill the entry hole of 32mm on the front wood

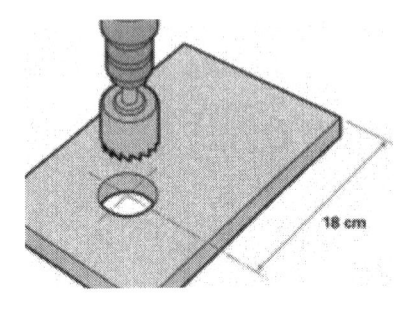

.Step 4: Mount the woods together using a wood glue or nail.

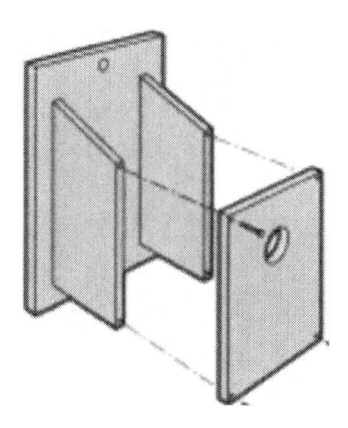

Step 5: For drainage, drill 10 mm of hole size underneath the birdhouse.

Step 6: Assemble it all together.

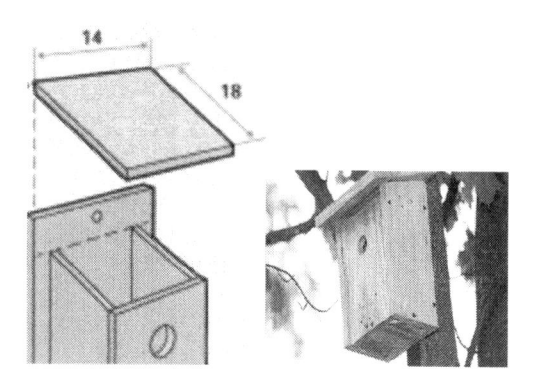

License Plates Birdhouse

This is a very exciting project. If you've got some license plate or something very much similar sticking around, this is a chance to put them to use. It is basically simple and not too different from other projects, except that it allows you to use an old license plate.

Supplies

- 1" ×8" × 4" cedar
- 1 1/8" drill bit
- ¼" drill bit
- Nails
- Screws
- License plate

Procedures

Step 1: Make a 4" ×6 ¼" cut for the sides

Step 2: Make a 25-degree cut using the 7" × 9" measurement for the front piece

Step 3: Drill your entry hole using the measurement 11/8", let the measurement of the distance between the bottom and the hole be about 4".

Step 4: Drill another tiny hole of ¼". make it 1" below the larger hole. This hole will be used to insert wood for perching.

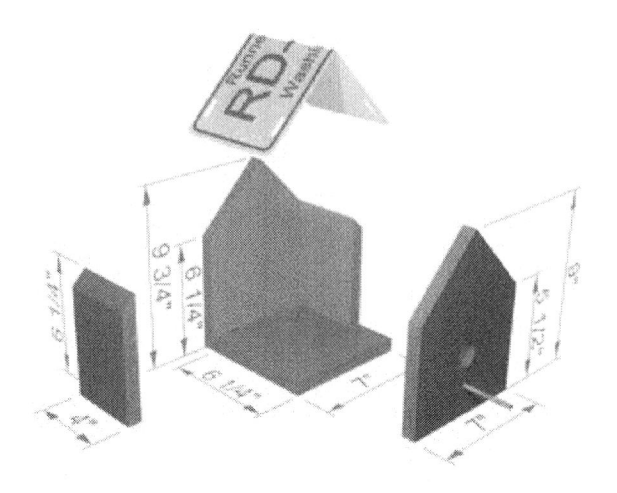

Step 5: Measure a 7" ×9 ¾" of the wood for the back, cutting at an angle of 40 degrees.

Step 6: Make a measurement of 6 ¼" × 7" before cutting. This piece is for the back.

Step 7: After making all the measurements and cuts, use the wood glue to assemble them together.

Step 8: Bend your license plate at the center and screw it into the top sides of the other woods. Place it carefully so that the bend would fit in the middle of the box. Screw the license into the wood and your birdhouse is very ready.

Songbird Birdhouse

This is a traditional and ancient birdhouse. One of the oldest there is. It is mainly built in the backyard for songbirds like the bluebird; this is why it comes with a little perch for the bird to perch when it doesn't want to be in the hole. Also, songbirds are not so big, so this birdhouse doesn't have to be big. A sizeable birdhouse is just fine. If you want a simple and small traditional birdhouse, then this is for you. It is not particularly attractive, but it is very functional and easy to make.

Supplies

- 1×6 lumber
- Brad's nails
- Glue
- Paint
- Hangers
- Jigsaw
- Hammer
- Drill
- Hole saw drill bit

Procedures

Step 1: Make the cuts; for the front and back, cut two 5" × 9" inches of the 1×6 lumber. For the two sides, cut 2 4" × 6" long pieces. For the roof, cut one 4 ½ "× 8 long for one side of the roof. Cut 5 ½ "× 8" for the other side. Measure and cut one long piece of 3 ½" × 4" of the lumber wood for the bottom. Make sure your measurements are accurate before you cut.

Step 2: Smooth the surface and the edges with a sand block. Sand the edges until they are smooth and round enough for you.

Step 3: Join the edges together to close up the birdhouse using wood glue as it is airtight and helps the wood to fit firmly.

Step 4: After gluing the first two woods together, hold them in a clamp to ensure that it is firm enough.

Step 5: You can go ahead to add nails to the structure to make it stronger. The components of the birdhouse should be aligned properly and the corner should be right- angled. Before hammering in your nails, ensure to drill pilot holes for the nails to pass through. Also, don't use too much force on the wood when hammering.

Step 6: Mark the entrance location and drill a hole of about 1 ¼" – 1 ½" to make a wide enough entrance.

Step 7: Fasten the roof of the house with nails on each side of the wood. Before fastening with nails, you can apply glue to make it more durable.

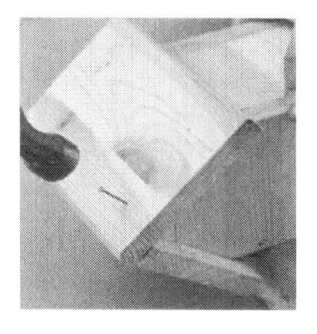

Step 8: Install the floor of the birdhouse using hinges; this is if you want it to be tight. But you could just hit it into the bottom so that you can open it at anytime you wish. That is your access door.

Step 9: Drill a tiny hole for the perch just 2" under the entrance of the birdhouse.

Step 10: Apply glue on a twig and insert it into the hole so that it stays firm and doesn't show on the inside. The perch should only be on the inside, so that the bird can still have good space to move around well.

Your birdhouse is ready.

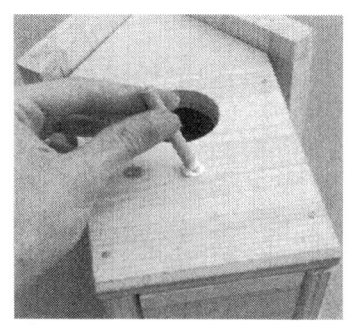

Sparrow Birdhouse Box

Statistics have it that the sparrow bird has declined in population by 50% since 1979. This was traced to the fact that sparrows usually rest under the leaves of houses, but most modern houses that are built today are far from being sparrow friendly. So, this has sent the birds into some sort of extinction. This birdhouse is made with a modification that impresses Sparrows is most friendly with the sparrows because it is made using a 12mm exterior plywood that can accommodate up to three separate breeding pairs of sparrows.

Supplies

- Any type of plywood
- Number 4 panel screws

Procedures

Step 1: Use the cutting list below to make your cuts; the top piece should be 44.5 × 21.5 cm, the bottom piece should be 15 × 38 cm, the front and back piece should be 19.5 × 40.5 cm and 25×40.5 cm, respectively. The left and right sides should be 15×25cm and 15×19.5cm, respectively.

Step 2: This is a triple birdhouse, so you would need to make extra cuts of two internal dividers to divide the birdhouse in sects. The internal divider should be measured and cut at 23.8×18.3 cm.

Step 3: You would also need to make a hanging support. Cut two pieces of wood for hanging support at 17×3 cm.

Step 4: Drill a 32mm hole in the left and right pieces for entry.

Step 5: Assemble all the pieces together using strong wood glue. You would have something like a book rack with 3 compartments.

Step 6: Drill the third hole on the front wood piece in the middle compartment. You can hang your birdhouse now at the roof top, as sparrows usually like to stay high from the ground.

Peanut Butter Birdhouse

You can take an attempt at creativity. You wouldn't harm anybody by just trying. It was an innovation that brought about the idea of using old license iron in building birdhouses. Here is another almost crazy idea, making a birdhouse of a peanut butter can! I love the idea that you can put to use old stuff that you aren't using instead of allowing them to be littered about.

Supplies

- Drill
- Chain and hook for hanging
- Sandpaper
- Bolt
- Soapy water
- Peanut jar
- Spray paint

Procedures

Step 1: Finish the peanut butter. I know this step sounds funny or unimportant, but you can't make a peanut butter birdhouse if there is still peanut butter inside. So, finish the butter, and wipe the inside clean with soapy water.

Step 2: Allow the jar to dry, then use a 1 ¼ inch drill bit to drill a hole in the center of the bottle. After which you sand it well with a good sander.

Step 3: Drill a smaller hole under the first one, and insert the bolt. Afterwards, screw the nut tight to make a secure hold.

Step 4: Use the small drill bit like the one you used above to make a little hole so you can insert a hanger for you to hang the peanut jar. Insert the brass hook into the hole and screw it into the hole. Cover the sticking out screw or bolt with hot glue so it doesn't affect the bird.

Step 5: Take off the cap and apply your paint to the body of the jar.

Step 6: Allow it to dry, then string through the bolts and hang the peanut jar.

Gourd Birdhouse

Birds are naturally attracted to natural things or structures like this gourd birdhouse. You can create a beautiful birdhouse just with this gourd. You don't need to adjust the shape; the birds are even attracted to this birdhouse because of its shape. All types of birds are attracted to this birdhouse, especially the woodpecker and purple martins. Don't think gourds are extinct; no, there are gourds available at the farmers' market.

Supplies

- Gourd
- Sandpaper
- Holesaw drill bit
- Leather lacing
- Latex paint
- Paintbrush

Procedures

Step 1: Find a clean and dry gourd. The gourd must have been drying for at least 3- 6 months. To check if the gourd is ready to be used, shake it lightly and pay attention to hear if the seeds rattle. If you hear some rattling noise, your birdhouse is perfectly dry. Well, gourds are not always perfectly clean, in the drying process, mold must have grown on the gourd; use tough sandpaper to clean the surface

Step 2: Locate the center of the gourd and drill a hole in the center. Ensure that the point you drilled the hole would not be facing up or down; it should be on the vertical level. After drilling, sand the edges of the hole with good sandpaper. Drill tiny holes at the bottom of the gourd for drainage. When drilling holes for a wren bird, ensure that the hole is quite small and the mounting height is 6 to 10 feet above the ground.

Also, for the purple martins, the birdhouse should be 10 to 15 feet above the ground. These are factors you have to consider.

Step 3: Clean the inside of the gourd with a spoon by scraping the rough edges. You will find some gourd seeds inside, be careful not to discard them while you clean the edges. You can plant them to grow new gourds.

Step 4: Use a 1/4" bit drill to drill in the bottom of the gourd three small holes for drainage. Also, add additional two holes at the top of the gourd for hanging.

Step 5: You could paint your birdhouse if you wish to using latex paint; lighter color keeps the house cool during summer. Use clear polyurethane to spray the outside as a sealant.

Step 6: Thread a leather lacing of your desired length through the drilled two holes forming the hanging strap. Hang it in your preferred location on a sturdy branch of a tree.

Your gourd birdhouse is ready.

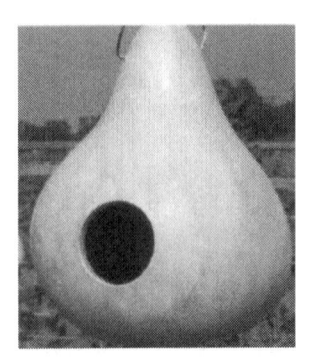

Natural Log Birdhouse

This is a more interesting and stress less project that allows you to create a

Who would think that a natural log can be put to so much good use? You can create a birdhouse from a natural log. It is a great birdhouse plan for native birds like owls, tree swallows, kestrels, woodpeckers, wrens, purple martins, bluebirds, chickadees, flickers, house finch, house sparrows, nuthatches. It won't be out of place to state that this is an all-bird's birdhouse. It can be used for all types of birds. The log doesn't just make the birdhouse look unique. It also provides extra warmth and insulation for the birds on cold and warm days alike. And the steps are so simple and straightforward.

Supplies

- Natural log
- Screw
- Handsaw
- Lumber
- Perch

Procedures

Step 1: Decide the roof type that you want. Do you want a flat roof or an angle A roof? It's your choice to make. If you would be using a flat roof, then you don't really need the lumber wood, you can create a flat roof, but make a straight cut on the log.

Step 2: Cut out the length of the birdhouse you want to have. Measure your log before cutting.

Step 3: Remove the center of the log using a handsaw.

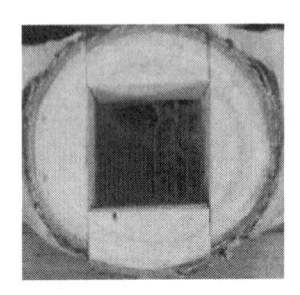

Step 4: Drill the center section for the entry hole, make it 4 cm wide.

Step 5: The center section will be disregarded like this when you use a handsaw. Drill pilot holes and insert screws to prevent the wood from splitting. Also, drill a hole for the perch.

Step 6: You can use the log, a license plate, or any other type of wood to make the roof. For the bottom of the birdhouse, make use of any type of wood.

Step 7: Your birdhouse is ready to be mounted.

Cardboard Birdhouse

If you are not really good at woodworking, you can still create a birdhouse on your own with the following steps. You can make this cardboard birdhouse with your kids. It requires very simple materials that are children-friendly. However, it is not to be used in rainy seasons, as the material is very weak and liable to get destroyed.

Supplies

- Carton or cardboard
- Perch

- Paint
- A bent wire hanger
- Dollhouse shingles

Procedures

Step 1: Cut a birdhouse and fold it in a cylindrical form.

Step 2: Cut out a circular roof for the cylinder and glue it to the cylinder. Also, cut out an entrance hole at the center.

Step 3: Place the shingles on the top of the roof and the wire hanger to hang the birdhouse. Also, cut out a small hole for the perch and insert the perch.

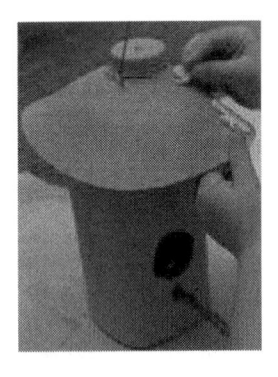

Step 4: Make your designs with stickers and colors. Your birdhouse is ready to be hanged.

The end... almost!

Hey! We've made it to the final chapter of this book, and I hope you've enjoyed it so far.

If you have not done so yet, I would be incredibly thankful if you could take just a minute to leave a quick review on Amazon

Reviews are not easy to come by, and as an independent author with a little marketing budget, I rely on you, my readers, to leave a short review on Amazon.

Even if it is just a sentence or two!

So if you really enjoyed this book, please...

\>\> Click here to leave a brief review on Amazon.

I truly appreciate your effort to leave your review, as it truly makes a huge difference.

Chapter 6

Common Problems With Building Birdhouses

1. When birds aren't visiting your birdhouse: The birdhouse is usually built to host birds, so when it happens that birds aren't really visiting the birdhouse, it becomes a serious problem. It is as though you invested all your time in a waste of activities. The birdhouse is useless in itself if it turns out that the birds for which you built it are not abiding in it. It can be very frustrating. So, how do you make them come? Your birdhouse can't just be accommodating dust for nothing?

   The first issue could be that there are no cavity-nesters in your backyard. There are only a few categories of birds that use birdhouses, so it could be possible that the birds around you are not those cavity-nesters. Also, it could be that there are no birds around your environs. If the second point is the case, you would have to consciously set up an impressively attractive atmosphere, especially around the birdhouse. You would have to look out for things that would impress the bird and attract it to the birdhouse. You can add bird feeders, water, and plants that you know would encourage the birds' presence. The more they find what they desire in your yard, the more they'll visit and check out the tools you have available, including the birdhouse.

2. Birds building nests before your birdhouses are ready: Well, you can't blame the birds; they can't just be dependent and waiting on a birdhouse that may not be made available. The birds have to survive on their own. They are not exactly dependent on humans. Hence, it is quite natural to expect birds to build their nest before you even start building your birdhouse. When you foresee this problem, it makes it easier for you to handle it well and make plans towards attracting the birds. Some persons go ahead to destroy the bird's nest, feeling or thinking that the next stop will be the birdhouse if they become homeless. Well, they get to realize it doesn't work that way. They might eventually come around to abide in your nest box, but it will be after a long time because your action would have chased them away. They would even seek to avoid that

territory for that time with the fear of danger, so destroying the nest is never the solution. First of all, you have to pay attention to the season before putting up the birdhouse. If you build the birdhouse during the spring season, you would miss the early nesters. They might still come around late during the end of the season. Hence, the best time to build the birdhouse is at the beginning and end of the spring season. Late winter is also a good time to consider building. Putting up the birdhouses early would attract your residents.

3. Birds usually ignore the birdhouse to nest somewhere else: One reason for such occurrence could be that your birdhouse is not made for that type of bird. It could be that the specification of the bird doesn't match the design of the birdhouse. Some birds are very sensitive down to the floor of the birdhouse, house shape, and other details. The main solution to this problem is studying to know the required specification for building a birdhouse of the species of bird that you intend to attract. Then, you can commence

your building according to specifications; floor width, height, color, shape, hole size, and many other things. You wouldn't live in a thatched house just because you need a place to shelter when you are certain that you can still stay somewhere better. The same applies to birds. Once you get the specification, place your birdhouse in a strategic position and all things being equal, your bird will definitely want to stay forever.

4. Birds build their nests at a location lower than the place where your birdhouse is located: This simply means that your placement is wrong. We have also said in the course of this book the importance of placing the birdhouse correctly. The location of the birdhouse is just as important as the size and shape of the box. Some birds prefer nesting in a higher location, while others would prefer to stay not too far from the ground. Wherever the bird chooses to stay would greatly determine the point they will nest. Birds have preferences for where they would stay and the fashion of the place, whether on a pole or a tree.

Understanding this preference would help you place your birdhouse in the proper or appropriate location.

5. Birds do not revisit the birdhouse: This happens because the birdhouse is dirty. Also, most times, birds like to build nests in their birdhouses. Hence, after the birds must have stayed for a season in the house, they might not be comfortable returning to the untidy place and staying there again. Therefore, it is very important that you have to clean the place every season if you want the birds to revisit. However, some birds could still build their nest with materials from older nests. This is why you must build a door to the birdhouse that can allow you to access it at any time and give you the grace to clean the birdhouse after the bird is gone, so it would feel comfortable in the next season when it returns. Just the same way you wouldn't want to move into a dirty house, even though it is free, the birds can deal with debris and droppings of dung from last season that is still very much in the birdhouse. In the long run, this also reduces

the possible risk of contamination from the dirt, old feces, decomposing feathers, amongst other things.

6. My painted and well-decorated birdhouse is not being used: Paints are toxic to birds, especially when the chemical is very harsh and toxic in itself. The birdhouse is definitely going to be toxic to them. So, they might have visited without your notice and feel uncomfortable then leave. Who wouldn't be attracted to beauty? Even animals are attracted to beauty and fine things, so when a bird is avoiding your decorated and well-designed birdhouse, it could mean that the paint is discomforting it or it doesn't feel so welcomed? This is why I laid emphasis on the fact that when building a birdhouse, you don't just build it to your taste, you have to put the other party into consideration because they are the ones to live in it. Hence, avoid paints with glitter or any other quirky accents, and opt for simple designs that are quite understated. Painting a birdhouse should be done in camouflage. In as much as you intend to draw the bird close to the birdhouse,

you should be careful not to also make designs that would be so shouty and attract predators. Hence, you must do a balanced and simple decoration. Also, avoid toxic paints or chemicals. Paints are not so necessary in birdhouse building, it is only important for the sake of beautifying the birdhouse and for the sake of warming the temperature on the inside.

7. Larger birds use my small bird birdhouse: This is one rare problem that can happen to just anyone. And sadly, sometimes, you might not have control over this problem. One thing that can lead to this is having inappropriate entrance hole. The size of the birdhouse isn't the only determining factor. If you are making a small-bird birdhouse, ensure that the entrance hole is small enough to accommodate just the size of birds that you intend to accommodate. However, if the hole happens to get bigger over time, there are simple ways to fix it.

8. Predators and invaders always attack my birdhouse: Actually, we have already made a comprehensive list of the things that could attract predators to your birdhouse; some of them are color or paint, location, entrance hole, perches and others. If you notice that the birdhouse is consistently being attacked by any of the predators we mentioned in the former chapters, then it is important that you check out the above possibilities. You may be the one attracting them in ignorance. First of all, ensure that the birdhouse is properly placed in the right location. In the long run, when predators consistently visit the birdhouse, the bird fears insecurity and tends to fly away. Security is very important to birds; hence if you must build them a birdhouse, ensure that it is secured and their safety won't be threatened. Remove any magnet that appears to be attracting these predators. You can remove the perches, scrape off the painting and reposition the birdhouse to a new location. Adding some baffles or guards could further help to intensify the security. Also, do well to keep all forms of pets like cats indoors. Also, go ahead to discourage

stray birds by putting protective guards. Every model should have adequate drainage and ventilation.

9. When strange insects occupy your birdhouse: Many people have reported that they found insects like bees in their birdhouse. They have mostly been found in birdhouses that once housed birds like Chickadees or Nuthatches. I tell you, this is a very frustrating experience that you don't want to experience. These insects usually take over the house after the birds must have left at the end of the nesting period. As harmless as it might seem, bees in birdhouses are a huge problem. They don't get to leave even when the real house owners return. They create a fuzz by their presence to not just the birds but the landowner. Bees are beneficial to the economy, but it can also be a big problem. Before they move into a house, they actually consider and plan their launch attack. Yeah, bees are that smart. Once they finally decide on the house, they don't wait to be welcomed, they just go ahead to launch their overtaking scheme on the house. Once they

arrive, the terrible downside is that they take time to leave because they usually come in a very large insurmountable group. As small as this creature might seem to you, the bee is a big monster to the chickadees. It is not just the bee, other insects like biting flies and giant spiders also pose a threat to the nuthatch, wren, chickadees. This is because they are quite small birds when compared to big birds; bees are like prey. So, the big question is, how do you keep these birds out of your house?

One sure thing you can do to solve this problem is clean your birdhouse on an annual basis. However, some persons argue that the bees are attracted to the birdhouse when it is clean. Another suggestion is to use insecticides to chase them away, but it is toxic in itself and makes the atmosphere unconducive for birds and their chicks when they return. Although the chemicals could dissipate quickly and become less harmful, how does it discourage the bees from returning until the birds begin nesting? It is quite a waste of resources, time and all. The best available option is to build the birdhouse with cedarwood. It has been proven that cedar is an insect repellant. If you happen to have built your birdhouse with wood other than the cedar wood, you don't have to discard it and build another one. You could add wood dust from cedar wood or wood shavings. Just spread them on the bottom of the birdhouse, it will make the birds feel more comfortable after it chases and repels all manner of insect from coming close to the birdhouse.

10. Placing your birdhouse in a highly visible place: The temptation to show everyone the beautiful construction you made could be a problem. Hence, it is common to want to place the birdhouse on the fence post, pillars, or any high and visible place where everyone will see it. This is not bad in itself, but most cavity nesters and songbirds would prefer a quiet space where they can easily come out and sing without having to compete to be heard. Mother birds would want to choose a location where she can rear and nest her chicks without stress or exposing them to danger. You could plant your birdhouse in a very quiet area of the wall or on the tree top where leaves would hide it. That appears to be the best place to position your birdhouse because it is where they

have naturally been nesting. This will also help you get occupants way earlier because the birds normally visit trees, so when they come around, they will certainly find a better accommodation and move in. though this isn't for all bids, some birds like the bluebirds love open fields. That is where you will certainly find them, so just research to know where the preferred bird you are planning to nest, where they constantly visit. However, you could still nest them in those places. Finally, avoid very dry and quiet or grassy areas. Predators like snakes are not far from there, so it is an exposure to attack.

11. Using poor construction materials: It is very important that you use high-quality materials to build because your birdhouse will most certainly be exposed to different harsh weather conditions you have no control over. The control you have is over the durability of the birdhouse, which is largely dependent on the material's quality. Look out for wood that would last longer than normal and has a great texture and quality. Your wood should be insect repellant. Also, the paint you

would be using would be non-toxic and applied to only the exterior.

12. Lack of ventilation and drainage: Just like every other house, elements move in and out of the box. You might be wondering why the entrance hole can't be a ventilation passage. The best channel of ventilation and drainage is tiny holes under the birdhouse. It directly reaches the bird. It circulates better. The drainage system allows for rainwater to pass and dry out.

Conclusion

Jason Ward made a popular quote that says, "birds have always had the ability to bring me out of a dark space and provide relief in bad times."

Having birds around you is indeed therapeutic and one way to make it possible is by building them a home near your home.

Building a birdhouse in itself is not difficult. You only have to create or adopt a creative plan according to the bird species you intend to attract.

Always remember that you have no one to impress other than your birds. They are the owners of the house, so if they would live in it, it has to be captivating to them.

By building a birdhouse, you get to help secure the ecosystem, as the birds are essential factors in the system and should be treated as such.

However, don't feel pressured to follow any particular style, you just have to understand the basics and necessary requirements of building a birdhouse.

Allow yourself to be creative but still follow the established principles. Ensure you use the right measurement for the birdhouse and its entrance hole to prevent predator attacks. You can further decide to use predator guards for extra safety. Also, maintain the correct mounting height; it all adds up to ensure safety. Remember, the birdhouse must provide comfort and security above all things.

Build a birdhouse today and watch nature reward you.

Printed in Great Britain
by Amazon